Medical Language
A SURVIVAL VOCABULARY

Jim Richey
Reading Specialist
Hayward Unified School District
Hayward, California

illustrated by Dennis Roberts

JB Janus Book Publishers
Hayward, California

Janus Survival Vocabulary Books

Banking Language

Clothing Language

Credit Language

Driver's License Language

Drugstore Language

Entertainment Language

Job Application Language

Medical Language

Restaurant Language

Sign Language (Books A, B, C, D)

Supermarket Language

International Standard Book Number: 0-915510-48-0

Printed in the United States of America.

45678900987654

Contents

Introduction

I had to go to a new medical center (MED i kuhl SENT er)* not too long ago. I had never been there before, so I didn't know what it was like.

I didn't know where to go. I didn't know whom to see. And I couldn't find anyone to tell me what I needed to know. I became so mixed up!

Then I noticed that there were signs all over the medical center. The signs showed where people should go. They showed where people could find certain kinds of medical help. They helped me find my way around the medical center.

After I left the center, I thought about what had happened to me. What if I hadn't known how to read the medical words on the signs? I might never have found the medical help I needed! I thought of how important it is for people to know the medical words that are often seen.

So I wrote this book. It can teach you medical words you might see at medical places or on medical forms. It can teach you medical words that are found on labels and in stores. Learn the words. They can help you the next time you need medical help.

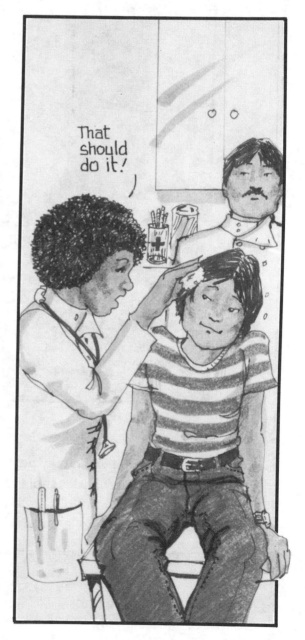

That should do it!

---

*You will see a respelling like this after each new word in this book. The respelling shows you how to say the word. To learn how to use the respellings, see page 48.

Unit One

Hospital   People go to a hospital (HAHS pit uhl) when they get hurt, are very sick, or need special medical care. Signs like the one in the picture are put on streets around hospitals.

Why are they put there?

_____

_____

_____

Pretest

- ☐ doctor
- ☐ nurse
- ☐ physician
- ☐ surgeon
- ☐ dentist
- ☐ DDS
- ☐ MD
- ☐ patient
- ☐ appointment
- ☐ emergency
- ☐ admissions
- ☐ registration
- ☐ ambulance
- ☐ laboratory
- ☐ therapy

You'd better see a physician about that eye.

Words and Meanings

Say the medical word out loud and read its meaning. Read the sentence that follows it. Then circle the medical word in the sentence. The first is done.

Doctor (DAHK ter): *person who treats sick or hurt people.*
The (doctor) made me well again.

Nurse (NERS): *person who takes care of sick or hurt people.*
The nurse cleaned the cut on my hand.

Physician (fuh ZISH uhn): *doctor of medicine.*
You'd better see a physician about that eye.

Surgeon (SER juhn): *doctor who can cut open and fix people's bodies.*
The surgeon fixed his bad heart.

Dentist (DENT uhst): *doctor who fixes teeth.*
The dentist put fillings in my teeth.

Same Words

Check the word in each row that is the same as the first word in the row. Go as fast as you can. Time yourself. The first is done.

Physician	Physical	Physician	Position
Dentist	Dental	Dented	Dentist
Nurse	Purse	Nurse	Norse
Doctor	Doctor	Dollar	Docker
Surgeon	Sturgeon	Surge	Surgeon

No. Correct _____

Time _____

Missing Vowels

To finish each word, fill in the missing vowels. Write the complete word on the line. The first is done.

nrs _____ *nurse* _____

dctr _____

dntst _____

physcn _____

srgn _____

Scrambled Letters

The letters in each word are mixed up. Write the letters so they spell a word from the list at the top of page 7. The first is done.

tedsnit _____ *dentist* _____

rodtoc _____

hspiyanic _____

eurns _____

runsego _____

Pick a Word

Underline the word that belongs in each sentence. Then write that word on the line. The first is done.

A _____ *surgeon* _____ fixes people's bodies.
    sturgeon   <u>surgeon</u>   dentist

A _____ fixes teeth.
    dentist   nurse   surgeon

A _____ treats sick or hurt people.
    dental   waiter   doctor

A _____ takes care of sick people.
    nurse   teacher   writer

A _____ is a medical doctor.
    sturgeon   physician   dental

I have an appointment to have my teeth cleaned.

Words and Meanings

Say the medical word out loud and read its meaning. Read the sentence that follows it. Then circle the medical word in the sentence.

DDS (DEE DEE ES): *a dentist.*

John Jones, DDS, is our dentist.

MD (EM DEE): *a medical doctor.*

Mary Smith, MD, is a surgeon.

Patient (PAY shuhnt): *one who gets medical or dental help.*

The doctor helps her patient.

Appointment (uh POINT muhnt): *a date and time to be at a certain place.*

I have an appointment to have my teeth cleaned.

Emergency (i MER juhn see): *a time when a sick or hurt person needs help right away.*

The doctors rushed to take care of the emergency.

Same Words

Check the word in each row that is the same as the first word in the row. Go as fast as you can. Time yourself.

Patient	Physician	Patent	Patient
MD	MR	MD	DM
Appointment	Apartment	Appointment	Pointing
Emergency	Emergency	Energy	Emerge
DDS	DSD	SDD	DDS

No. Correct _____

Time _____

Word Wheel

Begin at Start. Find the first word. Put a line between it and the next word. Find and mark the other words in the same way. Then write them on the lines below. The first is done.

_MD_

_____

_____

_____

_____

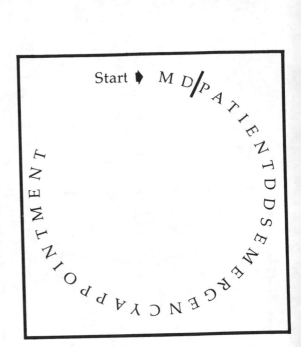

Start ➧ M D/P A T I E N T D D S E M E R G E N C Y A P P O I N T M E N T

Missing Ink

Complete each word by adding the missing parts to each letter. Then write that word on the line. The first is done.

DDS _____ _DDS_____

EMERGENCY _____

PATIENT _____

MD _____

APPOINTMENT _____

Pick a Word

Underline the word that belongs in each sentence. Then write that word on the line.

He made an _____ to see
a doctor.
    physician   energy   appointment

An _____ is a medical doctor.
      DDS   MD   DMV

This is an _____! Get a doctor
quickly!
    appointment   emergency   energy

A _____ is a dentist.
    DDS   MD   SDS

A _____ gets help from a
dentist or doctor.
    sturgeon   emergency   patient

Eating a good meal is part of my therapy.

Words and Meanings

Say the medical word out loud and read its meaning. Read the sentence that follows it. Then circle the medical word in the sentence.

Admissions (uhd MISH uhnz): *name of the office that lets people into a place.*

Patients entering the hospital must first go to Admissions.

Registration (rej uh STRAY shuhn): *filling in medical or hospital forms.*

New patients must go through a registration.

Ambulance (AM byuh luhns): *a van that takes sick or hurt people to a hospital.*

The ambulance rushed her to the hospital.

Laboratory (LAB uh ruh tor ee): *place where medical tests are done.*

The laboratory tests showed the patient was sick.

Therapy (THEHR uh pee): *something that is done to make a patient well.*

Eating a good meal is part of my therapy.

Same Words

Check the word in each row that is the same as the first word in the row. Go as fast as you can. Time yourself.

Laboratory	Lavatory	Laboratory	Largely
Admissions	Admissions	Additions	Emissions
Therapy	Theology	Theory	Therapy
Ambulance	Imbalance	Ambulance	Amicable
Registration	Restoration	Registration	Region

No. Correct _____

Time _____

Letter Squares

The letters in each square spell a word from the list at the top of page 11. Write that word below the square. The first is done.

therapy

Missing Ink

Complete each word by adding the missing parts to each letter. Then write that word on the line.

AMBULANCE _____

ADMISSIONS _____

THERAPY _____

LABORATORY _____

REGISTRATION _____

Pick a Word

Underline the word that belongs in each sentence. Then write that word on the line.

The patient rode in the _____.
    ambulance   emergency   surgeon

_____ helps make him well.
    Admissions   Registration   Therapy

The _____ makes medical tests.
    appointment   laboratory   dentist

Hospitals have _____ offices.
    admissions   sturgeon   emerge

At the _____ desk, he filled in some forms.
    position   registration   emissions

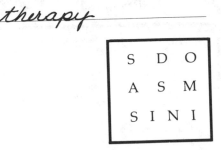

Unit One

Review

The 15 words listed below are hidden in the puzzle. Each word is printed in a straight line. But it may read across, up, down, backwards, or on a slant. Some words overlap. Circle each word as you find it in the puzzle. Then cross it off the list. One is done.

DOCTOR
NURSE
PHYSICIAN
SURGEON
DENTIST
DDS
~~MD~~
PATIENT

APPOINTMENT
EMERGENCY
ADMISSIONS
REGISTRATION
AMBULANCE
LABORATORY
THERAPY

```
A  L  A  P  P  O  I  N  T  M  E  N  T
M  A  T  T  H  E  R  A  P  Y  Q  U  I
B  B  C  K  Y  N  B  R  O  N  W  A  O
A  O  X  J  S  U  U  M  P  D  E  N  O
M  R  E  G  I  S  T  R  A  T  I  O  N
B  A  V  T  C  R  E  L  S  A  Z  E  Y
U  T  C  A  I  T  A  D  P  E  D  G  P
L  O  P  R  A  E  D  S  I  O  D  R  A
A  R  E  N  N  T  E  A  C  E  R  U  T
N  Y  G  E  D  E  N  T  I  S  T  S  I
C  N  C  Y  T  H  O  B  A  W  T  L  E
E  A  E  M  E  R  G  E  N  C  Y  M  N
A  A  D  M  I  S  S  I  O  N  S  S  T
```

Test

Put **+** by each sentence that is true. Put **0** by each sentence that is not true.

_____ 1. An MD is a dentist.

_____ 2. A nurse is a surgeon.

_____ 3. Forms are filled in during registration.

_____ 4. A physician is a doctor.

_____ 5. A DDS works in an admissions office.

_____ 6. Therapy helps people get better.

_____ 7. A patient rides in an ambulance.

_____ 8. A laboratory gives medical tests.

_____ 9. Hospitals don't handle emergency cases.

_____ 10. An appointment is a medical test.

13

Unit Two

Medical Service Directory   A medical service (SERV uhs) directory (duh REK tuh ree) helps people use places such as hospitals. It tells where to find different kinds of medical help, what phone numbers to call, and who the doctors are. What kind of help is the person above looking for?

_____

_____

Pretest

- ☐ physical examination
- ☐ positive
- ☐ negative
- ☐ allergy
- ☐ optical
- ☐ operation
- ☐ injury
- ☐ insurance
- ☐ health plan
- ☐ dental plan
- ☐ radiology
- ☐ pediatrics
- ☐ urology
- ☐ obstetrics
- ☐ gynecology

His allergy makes him sneeze whenever he is near a cat.

Words and Meanings

Say the medical word out loud and read its meaning. Read the sentence that follows it. Then circle the medical word in the sentence.

Physical Examination (FIZ i kuhl ig zam uh NAY shuhn): *a medical checkup of a person's body.*
The doctor gave me a physical examination.

Positive (PAHZ uht iv): *test result that shows someone needs medical help.*
He had to go to the hospital because his test result was positive.

Negative (NEG uht iv): *test result that shows someone is not sick.*
Your test result is negative, so you won't need any medicine.

Allergy (AL er jee): *a sickness that is caused by being close to certain things, such as fur.*
His allergy makes him sneeze whenever he is near a cat.

Optical (AHP ti kuhl): *anything to do with eyeglasses, contact lenses, etc.*
She got eyeglasses in the optical department.

Same Words

Check the word or phrase in each row that is the same as the first word or phrase in the row. Go as fast as you can. Time yourself.

Allergy	Already	Allergy
Negative	Negotiate	Negative
Physical Examination	Physical Education	Physical Examination
Optical	Optimal	Optical
Positive	Positive	Posture

No. Correct _____

Time _____

15

Word Wheel

Begin at Start. Find the first word or phrase. Put a line between it and the next word or phrase. Find and mark the other words or phrases in the same way. Then write them on the lines below.

_____

_____

_____

_____

_____

Missing Vowels

To finish each word, fill in the missing vowels. Write the complete word on the line.

llrgy _____

ptcl _____

physcl xmntn _____

pstv _____

ngtv _____

Pick a Word

Underline the word or phrase that belongs in each sentence. Then write that word or phrase on the line.

The test result was _____ .

     therapy   positive   emergency

She went to the _____ department
for eyeglasses.

     optical   ambulance   admissions

A _____ is
a health checkup.

     nurse   positive   physical examination

The test result was _____ . It
meant the patient was not ill.

     position   optical   negative

The _____ made his skin sore.

     appointment   allergy   admissions

I wish my insurance covered his doctor's bills.

Words and Meanings

Say the medical word out loud and read its meaning. Read the sentence that follows it. Then circle the medical word in the sentence.

Operation (ahp uh RAY shuhn): *cutting open the body in order to fix it.*

The operation was done by a surgeon.

Injury (INJ uh ree): *harm or hurt that is done to the body.*

The fall gave her a head injury.

Insurance (in SHUR uhns): *a plan that pays out money for such things as medical bills.*

I wish my insurance covered his doctor's bills.

Health Plan (HELTH PLAN): *insurance that pays medical bills.*

My health plan paid most of my hospital bills.

Dental Plan (DENT uhl PLAN): *insurance that pays dentists' bills.*

His dental plan paid for all the work that was done on his teeth.

Same Words

Check the word or phrase in each row that is the same as the first word or phrase in the row. Go as fast as you can. Time yourself.

Health Plan	Help Paint	Health Plan	Hot Pan
Operation	Operator	Optical	Operation
Insurance	Innocence	Insurance	Injury
Dental Plan	Dented Pan	Dental Plan	Rental Plan
Injury	Injury	Industry	Infantry

No. Correct _____

Time _____

Letter Squares

The letters in each square spell a word or phrase from the list at the top of page 17. Write that word or phrase below the square.

Missing Ink

Complete each word by adding the missing parts to each letter. Then write that word on the line.

DENTAL PLAN _____

_____

INJURY _____

OPERATION _____

INSURANCE _____

HEALTH PLAN _____

_____

Pick a Word

Underline the word or phrase that belongs in each sentence. Then write that word or phrase on the line.

People can get _____ to help pay hospital bills.

    injury   admissions   insurance

A _____ pays for medical help.

    health plan   hot pan   registration

The surgeon did an _____ on his leg.

    optical   operation   appointment

A _____ pays dentists' bills.

    registration   dental plan   laboratory

An _____ is a hurt.

    injury   optical   operation

N N C
R I U
S A E

_____

U J I
R
N Y

_____

N D E
T A L
P A N L

_____

_____

N T R
O A O
P E I

_____

E H A
L T H
N P L A

_____

_____

The pediatrics department only treats persons up to 16 years of age.

Words and Meanings

Say the medical word out loud and read its meaning. Read the sentence that follows it. Then circle the medical word in the sentence.

Radiology (rayd ee AHL uh jee): *place where X rays are taken.*

She got an X ray in the room marked "Radiology."

Pediatrics (peed ee A triks): *place that gives medical care to children only.*

The pediatrics department only treats persons up to 16 years of age.

Urology (yu RAHL uh jee): *place that can give special medical care to men.*

He saw a doctor in the urology department.

Obstetrics (uhb STE triks): *place that gives medical care to women having babies.*

She went to the obstetrics department before she had her baby.

Gynecology (gighn uh KAHL uh jee): *place that gives special medical care to women only.*

She had an examination in the gynecology department.

Same Words

Check the word in each row that is the same as the first word in the row. Go as fast as you can. Time yourself.

Gynecology	Gymnasium	Geology	Gynecology
Urology	Urology	Allergy	Usury
Pediatrics	Pedestrians	Pediatrics	Podiatrists
Radiology	Radioactive	Radiology	Rationality
Obstetrics	Obstructs	Obscures	Obstetrics

No. Correct _____

Time _____

19

Missing Vowels

To finish each word, fill in the missing vowels. Write the complete word on the line.

pdtrcs _____

bsttrcs _____

gynclgy _____

rdlgy _____

rlgy _____

Scrambled Letters

The letters in each word are mixed up. Write the letters so they spell a word from the list at the top of page 19.

goluryo _____

stricobset _____

gygyloneco _____

giolradoy _____

irtsiacped _____

Pick a Word

Underline the word that belongs in each sentence. Then write that word on the line.

The _____ department gives
  special medical care to men.
     obstetrics   pediatrics   urology

The _____ department gives
  medical care to women who are having babies.
     allergy   obstetrics   radiology

The _____ department
  takes X rays.
     radiology   registration   urology

The _____ department gives
  medical care to children only.
     urology   obstetrics   pediatrics

The _____ department gives
  medical care to women only.
     urology   pediatrics   gynecology

Unit Two

Review

The 15 words and phrases from the list on page 14 fit into this puzzle. They go across and down. The clues below will help you fill in the puzzle. The first is done.

Across

1. Department that treats women only
5. Something a surgeon does
9. A hurt
10. A kind of sickness
13. Department for women having babies
14. Department that fits eyeglasses
15. Something that pays dentists

Down

2. Test result that shows nothing is wrong
3. Department men can go to for special care
4. Test result that shows a person may need medical care
6. Health checkup
7. Something that pays doctors
8. Department that treats children
11. Department that takes X rays
12. Something that pays for medical care

Test

Answer the questions below. Write **Yes** or **No** in front of each one.

_____ 1. Can a urology place help men?
_____ 2. Is a health plan a kind of insurance?
_____ 3. Is a physical examination the same as a checkup?
_____ 4. Does a positive test result show illness?
_____ 5. Is *optical* a kind of allergy?

_____ 6. Is *pediatrics* the same as *obstetrics?*
_____ 7. Does a negative test mean that someone should get medical care?
_____ 8. Do dental plans pay dentists' bills?
_____ 9. Does a radiology place take X rays?
_____ 10. Can men get special help in the gynecology department?

Unit Three

Clinic A clinic (KLIN ik) is a place where people can get medical care. There are many different kinds of clinics. Some clinics are part of hospitals; some are not. Some give several kinds of medical help; some give only one kind. What kind of medical help does the clinic above give?

_____

Pretest

- ☐ immunizations
- ☐ disease
- ☐ vaccine
- ☐ booster
- ☐ health history

- ☐ tetanus
- ☐ measles
- ☐ mumps
- ☐ tuberculosis
- ☐ asthma

- ☐ poliomyelitis
- ☐ diabetes
- ☐ rheumatic fever
- ☐ hernia
- ☐ sinus

Please write down your health history.

Words and Meanings

Say the medical word out loud and read its meaning. Read the sentence that follows it. Then circle the medical word in the sentence.

Immunizations (im yuh nuh ZAY shuhnz): *shots that are given to keep people from getting sick.*
What immunizations did the doctor give you?

Disease (diz EEZ): *an illness.*
The doctor gave him a shot for the disease.

Vaccine (vak SEEN): *medicine that keeps people from getting a certain disease.*
This vaccine keeps you from getting smallpox.

Booster (BOO ster): *another dose of vaccine.*
A booster shot makes your immunization last a longer time.

Health History (HELTH HIS tuh ree): *a list of a person's illnesses and immunizations.*
Please write down your health history.

Same Words

Check the word or phrase in each row that is the same as the first word or phrase in the row. Go as fast as you can. Time yourself.

Health History	Health Plan	Health History
Vaccine	Vaccine	Vacation
Disease	Disaster	Disease
Immunizations	Admissions	Immunizations
Booster	Booster	Rooster

No. Correct _____

Time _____

Letter Squares

The letters in each square spell a word or phrase from the list at the top of page 23. Write that word or phrase below the square.

<table>
<tr><td>O B</td></tr>
<tr><td>T E R</td></tr>
<tr><td>S O</td></tr>
</table>

Missing Ink

Complete each word by adding the missing parts to each letter. Then write that word on the line.

DISEASE _____

IMMUNIZATIONS _____

HEALTH

   HISTORY _____

_____

VACCINE _____

BOOSTER _____

<table>
<tr><td>A I Z I</td></tr>
<tr><td>M U M N</td></tr>
<tr><td>I T O N S</td></tr>
</table>

<table>
<tr><td>E A</td></tr>
<tr><td>E D</td></tr>
<tr><td>I S S</td></tr>
</table>

Pick a Word

Underline the word or phrase that belongs in each sentence. Then write that word or phrase on the line.

A _____ is an illness.

    disease   urology   negative

_____ keep people from getting sick.

Immigrants   Immunizations   Immersions

A _____ helps keep people well.

    vacillate   vocation   vaccine

A _____ tells about a person's health.

health history   health plan   heat wave

A _____ makes an immunization last longer.

    broker   boxer   booster

<table>
<tr><td>L H E A</td></tr>
<tr><td>T H I H</td></tr>
<tr><td>S O</td></tr>
<tr><td>T R Y</td></tr>
</table>

<table>
<tr><td>N E C</td></tr>
<tr><td>C I V A</td></tr>
</table>

Red spots on the face and on the body are a sign of measles.

Words and Meanings

Say the medical word out loud and read its meaning. Read the sentence that follows it. Then circle the medical word in the sentence.

Tetanus (TET uhn uhs): *also called lockjaw; a disease that can cause death.*

Tetanus is caused by certain germs that live in dirt.

Measles (MEE zuhlz): *a disease children can get.*

Red spots on the face and on the body are a sign of measles.

Mumps (MUHMPS): *a disease that makes the cheeks swell up.*

A person finds it hard to chew when she or he has mumps.

Tuberculosis (tu ber kyuh LOH suhs): *also called TB; a lung disease that is caused by germs.*

You can take a test to see if you have tuberculosis.

Asthma (AZ muh): *a sickness of the lungs that is often caused by an allergy.*

People with asthma have a hard time breathing.

Same Words

Check the word in each row that is the same as the first word in the row. Go as fast as you can. Time yourself.

Mumps	Mopes	Mumps
Asthma	Asthma	Aster
Measles	Needles	Measles
Tetanus	Tennis	Tetanus
Tuberculosis	Tuberculosis	Tuberoses

No. Correct _____

Time _____

Word Wheel

Begin at Start. Find the first word. Put a line between it and the next word. Find and mark the other words in the same way. Then write them on the lines below.

_____

_____

_____

_____

_____

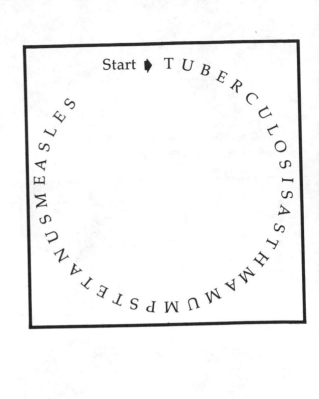

Start ▶ TUBERCULOSISASTHMAMUMPSTETANUSMEASLES

Scrambled Letters

The letters in each word are mixed up. Write the letters so they spell a word from the list at the top of page 25.

sumpm _____

hamtas _____

setanut _____

butrilocesus _____

slesmea _____

Pick a Word

Underline the word that belongs in each sentence. Then write that word on the line.

_____ cause swelling and pain.

    Optical   Mumps   Mopes

_____ is a lung disease.

  Tuberculosis   Tuberoses   Vaccine

_____ is also called lockjaw.

    Urology   Measles   Tetanus

_____ can be caused by an allergy.

  Measles   Booster   Asthma

Red spots are a sign of _____ .

  operation   measles   obstetrics

I can't smell anything because of my sinus.

Words and Meanings

Say the medical word out loud and read its meaning. Read the sentence that follows it. Then circle the medical word in the sentence.

Poliomyelitis (POH lee oh migh uh LIGHT uhs): *also called polio; a disease that can cripple the body.*
You can get a vaccine for poliomyelitis.

Diabetes (digh uh BEET uhs): *a disease where certain organs in the body don't work correctly.*
People with diabetes must be very careful about what they eat.

Rheumatic Fever (ru MAT ik FEE ver): *a harmful disease that children and young people get.*
Rheumatic fever sometimes hurts the heart.

Hernia (HER nee uh): *a part inside the body that has been pulled out of its place.*
The operation fixed his hernia.

Sinus (SIGH nuhs): *short word for sinusitis; a sickness that makes the inside of the nose swell up.*
I can't smell anything because of my sinus.

Same Words

Check the word or phrase in each row that is the same as the first word or phrase in the row. Go as fast as you can. Time yourself.

Hernia	Hernia	Heron
Diabetes	Diagrams	Diabetes
Sinus	Sinus	Signs
Rheumatic Fever	Rheumatism	Rheumatic Fever
Poliomyelitis	Polyonymous	Poliomyelitis

No. Correct _____

Time _____

Letter Squares

The letters in each square spell a word or phrase from the list at the top of page 27. Write that word or phrase below the square.

Missing Vowels

To finish each word, fill in the missing vowels. Write the complete word on the line.

rhmtc fvr _____

hrn _____

dbts _____

plmylts _____

sns _____

Pick a Word

Underline the word or phrase that belongs in each sentence. Then write that word or phrase on the line.

Polio is a short name for _____.
   photograph   poliomyelitis   water polo

An operation can sometimes fix a _____.
    hernia   booster   therapy

_____ can hurt a child.
  Admissions   Insurance   Rheumatic fever

Her nose swells up when she has _____.
    sinus   optical   registration

A person with _____ must eat carefully.
    negative   diabetes   vaccine

E T B
D I
A S E

_____

N S
I S U

_____

R H E
N A I

_____

M P O L
Y I O
L E T
I S I

_____

M U R H
E A T
I C F
R V E E

_____

Unit Three

Review

The 15 words and phrases from the list on page 22 fit into this puzzle. The first and last letters of each one are given. The letters where they cross are also given. Fill in the missing letters. Don't look back unless you have to. One is done for you.

Test

Put **+** by each sentence that is true. Put **0** by each sentence that is not true.

_____ 1. A health history tells about immunizations.

_____ 2. Certain germs in dirt cause tetanus.

_____ 3. Only men get rheumatic fever.

_____ 4. Asthma can sometimes be caused by allergies.

_____ 5. Measles is the same as mumps.

_____ 6. Sinus is a kind of hernia.

_____ 7. A test can show if a person has tuberculosis.

_____ 8. A booster makes a vaccine last longer.

_____ 9. *Polio* is short for *poliomyelitis*.

_____ 10. Diabetes is a disease.

29

Unit Four

First Aid   When someone needs medical help fast, she or he may need first aid. That's why many people keep first-aid kits handy. These kits are packed with things that might be needed if someone gets hurt or sick. Where might you keep such a kit?

_____

_____

Pretest

- ☐ pharmacy
- ☐ treatment
- ☐ antiseptic
- ☐ sterile
- ☐ medicated
- ☐ bandages
- ☐ cotton
- ☐ compress
- ☐ gauze pads
- ☐ adhesive tape
- ☐ thermometer
- ☐ alcohol
- ☐ ointment
- ☐ elastic
- ☐ scissors

Are the doctor's tools sterile?

Words and Meanings

Say the medical word out loud and read its meaning. Read the sentence that follows it. Then circle the medical word in the sentence.

Pharmacy (FAHR muh see): *place to get medicine; a drugstore.*
I bought these pills at the pharmacy.

Treatment (TREET muhnt): *medical help.*
She went to a clinic for treatment.

Antiseptic (ant uh SEP tik): *medicine that kills germs.*
He cleaned the cut with an antiseptic.

Sterile (STER uhl): *free from harmful germs.*
Are the doctor's tools sterile?

Medicated (MED uh kayt uhd): *having medicine in it.*
The doctor washed his hands with medicated soap.

Same Words

Check the word in each row that is the same as the first word in the row. Go as fast as you can. Time yourself.

Treatment	Tetanus	Treatment	Treating
Sterile	Sterile	Sterilize	Stern
Antiseptic	Antiserum	Antiseptic	Antacid
Medicated	Medicine	Medicated	Medical
Pharmacy	Pharmacy	Physician	Physical

No. Correct _____

Time _____

Word Wheel

Begin at Start. Find the first word. Put a line between it and the next word. Find and mark the other words in the same way. Then write them on the lines below.

_____

_____

_____

_____

_____

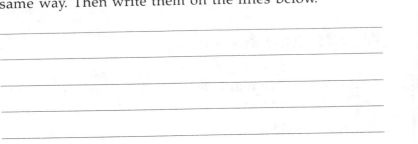

Start ▶ S T E R I L E M E D I C A T E D P H A R M A C Y A N T I S E P T I C T R E A T M E N T

Missing Ink

Complete each word by adding the missing parts to each letter. Then write that word on the line.

PHAPMACY _____

TREATMENT _____

MEDICATED _____

STERILE _____

ANTISEPTIC _____

Pick a Word

Underline the word that belongs in each sentence. Then write that word on the line.

Doctors give _____ for diseases.
    hernia   optical   treatment

The doctor's tools were _____ .
    sterile   negative   operation

An _____ kills germs.
    allergy   antiseptic   injury

A _____ sells medicine.
    laboratory   pharmacy   directory

Something that is _____ has medicine in it.
    optical   negative   medicated

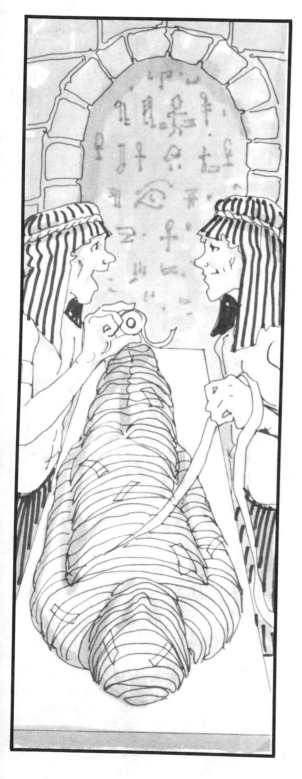

Adhesive tape keeps the bandages from coming off.

Words and Meanings

Say the medical word out loud and read its meaning. Read the sentence that follows it. Then circle the medical word in the sentence.

Bandages (BAN dij uhz): *pieces of cloth used to cover an injury.*

The doctor put bandages on his cuts.

Cotton (KAHT uhn): *soft, fuzzy stuff used to wipe things with.*

The nurse wiped his skin with a piece of cotton.

Compress (KAHM pres): *a pad or a folded cloth.*

She pressed on the cut with a compress.

Gauze Pads (GAWZ PADS): *folded pieces of soft, thin cloth.*

The nurse put gauze pads over the burns.

Adhesive Tape (ad HEE siv TAYP): *tape that can stick to the skin.*

Adhesive tape keeps the bandages from coming off.

Same Words

Check the word or phrase in each row that is the same as the first word or phrase in the row. Go as fast as you can. Time yourself.

Compress	Compass	Compress
Gauze Pads	Gauze Pads	Gauge Pins
Cotton	Gotten	Cotton
Bandages	Bandages	Bandana
Adhesive Tape	Adhesive Tape	Allergy Type

No. Correct _____

Time _____

Letter Squares

The letters in each square spell a word or phrase from the list at the top of page 33. Write that word or phrase below the square.

Missing Ink

Complete each word by adding the missing parts to each letter. Then write that word on the line.

BANDAGES _____

COTTON _____

ADHESIVE _____

TAPE _____

COMPRESS _____

GAUZE PADS _____

Pick a Word

Underline the word or phrase that belongs in each sentence. Then write that word or phrase on the line.

He put alcohol on a piece of _____ .
    polio   mumps   cotton

The nurse pressed a _____ on the leg.
    compress   positive   pharmacy

The _____ covered the injury.
    bandages   negatives   pediatrics

_____ are folded pieces of soft, thin cloth.
    Opticals   Sinus   Gauze pads

_____ sticks to the skin.
    Medicated   Adhesive tape   Asthma

The doctor said to put an elastic bandage around my knee.

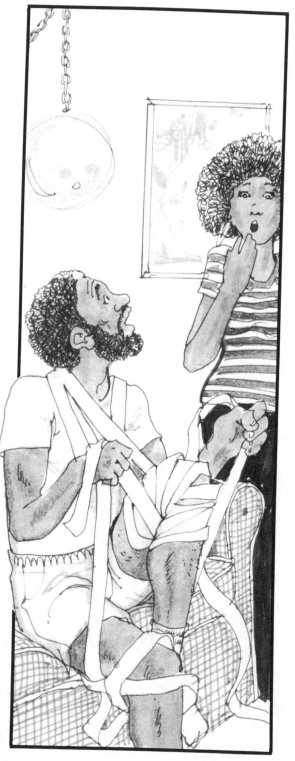

Words and Meanings

Say the medical word out loud and read its meaning. Read the sentence that follows it. Then circle the medical word in the sentence.

Thermometer (THER mahm uht er): *something that measures how hot a person's body is.*
The nurse put a thermometer in his mouth.

Alcohol (AL kuh hawl): *an antiseptic.*
She put alcohol on the sore.

Ointment (OINT muhnt): *medicine for the skin.*
He put ointment on the rash.

Elastic (i LAS tik): *easy to stretch.*
The doctor said to put an elastic bandage around my knee.

Scissors (SIZ erz): *a cutting tool.*
She cut the bandage with the scissors.

Same Words

Check the word in each row that is the same as the first word in the row. Go as fast as you can. Time yourself.

Ointment	Ointment	Optical	Obstetrics
Scissors	Sinus	Sterile	Scissors
Alcohol	Allergy	Alcohol	Alkaloid
Elastic	Elastic	Alaska	Eraser
Thermometer	Themselves	Thermos	Thermometer

No. Correct _____

Time _____

35

Missing Vowels

To finish each word, fill in the missing vowels. Write the complete word on the line.

scssrs _____

ntmnt _____

thrmmtr _____

lstc _____

lchl _____

Scrambled Letters

The letters in each word are mixed up. Write the letters so they spell a word from the list at the top of page 35.

lochalo _____

ciastel _____

rthemomtere _____

tinotenm _____

sorsicss _____

Pick a Word

Underline the word that belongs in each sentence. Then write that word on the line.

_____ is an antiseptic.

    Measles   Alcohol   Elastic

_____ is medicine for the skin.

    Ointment   Diabetes   Allergy

_____ means easy to stretch.

    Boosters   Elastic   Tetanus

A _____ measures how hot a person's body is.

  appointment   tuberculosis   thermometer

_____ are used to cut things.

    Scissors   Obstetrics   Sterile

Unit Four

Review

The 15 words and phrases from the list on page 30 fit into this puzzle. They go across and down. The sentences below will help you fill in the puzzle. Write the correct word or phrase in each sentence. Then write it in the puzzle. One is done.

Across

3. _Gauze pads_ are sometimes put over burns.

5. A _____ measures how hot someone's body is.

6. An _____ kills germs.

8. Something that is _____ has medicine in it.

10. A _____ can be used to press on the body.

12. Something that is _____ will stretch.

15. Doctors give _____ to patients.

Down

1. A drugstore is a _____.

2. _____ cover injuries.

4. _____ sticks to the skin.

7. _____ can cut tape.

9. _____ is an antiseptic.

11. _____ is used on skin.

13. A doctor's tools are _____.

14. _____ is used to clean cuts.

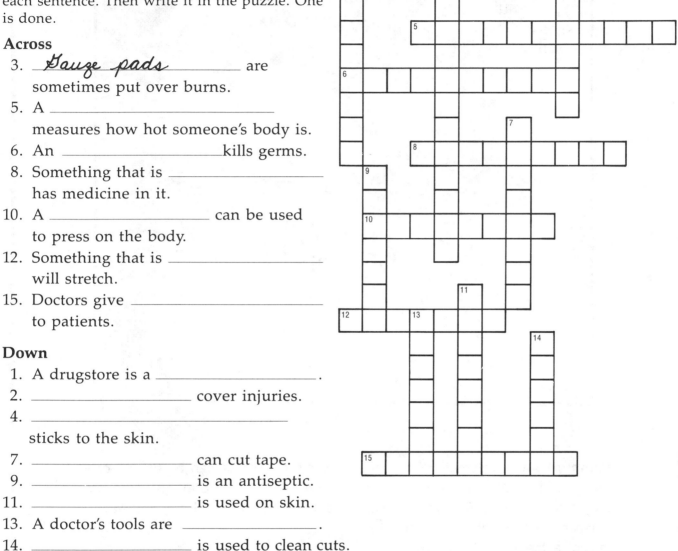

Test

Answer the questions below. Write **Yes** or **No** in front of each of them.

_____ 1. Are some soaps medicated?

_____ 2. Are scissors used for cutting?

_____ 3. Is cotton an adhesive tape?

_____ 4. Is alcohol an antiseptic?

_____ 5. Is an ointment a bandage?

_____ 6. Does *sterile* mean elastic?

_____ 7. Does *treatment* mean medical help?

_____ 8. Are gauze pads a kind of pill?

_____ 9. Is a thermometer a compress?

_____ 10. Is *pharmacy* the same as *insurance*?

Unit Five

Prescriptions Sometimes doctors or dentists will give a patient a prescription (pri SKRIP shuhn). The prescription tells the pharmacy what medicine the patient should get and how much of it she or he should take.

Some medicines can be bought only with such a prescription. Why are some medicines sold only that way?

_____

_____

Pretest

- ☐ chronic
- ☐ cough
- ☐ convulsion
- ☐ exhaustion
- ☐ bleeding
- ☐ pain
- ☐ acute
- ☐ fever
- ☐ headache
- ☐ dizziness
- ☐ vomiting
- ☐ unconscious
- ☐ infection
- ☐ nausea
- ☐ nervous
- ☐ wound
- ☐ inflammation
- ☐ capsule
- ☐ tablet
- ☐ addictive

A rest will get rid of your exhaustion.

Words and Meanings

Say the medical word out loud and read its meaning. Read the sentence that follows it. Then circle the medical word in the sentence.

Chronic (KRAHN ik): *lasting a long time; happening again and again.*

He was sick for months because of chronic colds.

Cough (KAWF): *a way to force air out the throat.*

The cold made her cough a lot.

Convulsion (kuhn VUHL shuhn): *shaking that is hard to stop; a fit.*

The medicine stopped his convulsion.

Exhaustion (ig ZAWS chuhn): *being very tired or worn out.*

A rest will get rid of your exhaustion.

Bleeding (BLEED ing): *losing blood.*

She was bleeding from the cut.

Same Words

Check the word in each row that is the same as the first word in the row. Go as fast as you can. Time yourself.

Convulsion	Convert	Condition	Convulsion
Bleeding	Beeping	Bleeding	Blending
Cough	Cough	Cuff	Rough
Chronic	Catholic	Chronic	Chronicle
Exhaustion	Exhalation	Expansion	Exhaustion

No. Correct _____

Time _____

Word Wheel

Begin at Start. Find the first word. Put a line between it and the next word. Find and mark the other words in the same way. Then write them on the lines below.

_____

_____

_____

_____

_____

Scrambled Letters

The letters in each word are mixed up. Write the letters so they spell a word from the list at the top of page 39.

houcg _____

hxeaustino _____

roncich _____

nocvulnois _____

ebledign _____

Pick a Word

Underline the word that belongs in each sentence. Then write that word on the line.

The doctor stopped the _____ .
    bleeding   cotton   ointment

The man who had the _____ was taken
to the emergency hospital.
    registration   radiology   convulsion

Her allergy made her _____ .
    gauze   cough   elastic

His _____ comes from working too hard.
    positive   exhaustion   treatment

She needs medicine for her _____ cold.
    chronic   sterile   capsule

Your job must give you a headache.

Words and Meanings

Say the medical word out loud and read its meaning. Read the sentence that follows it. Then circle the medical word in the sentence.

Pain (PAYN): *hurt.*
  The patient had a pain in his side.
Acute (uh KYOOT): *very sharp or strong.*
  He had an acute pain in his chest.
Fever (FEE ver): *high body heat.*
  The sick child had a fever.
Headache (HED ayk): *a pain in the head.*
  Your job must give you a headache.
Dizziness (DIZ ee nuhs): *spinning feeling in the head.*
  Dizziness caused her to fall down.

Same Words

Check the word in each row that is the same as the first word in the row. Go as fast as you can. Time yourself.

Headache	Health	Headache	Heartache
Dizziness	Diabetes	Dizzy	Dizziness
Acute	Accurate	Acute	Accent
Fever	Fever	Feeder	Fervor
Pain	Rain	Pane	Pain

No. Correct _____

Time _____

41

Letter Squares

The letters in each square spell a word from the list at the top of page 41. Write that word below the square.

Missing Vowels

To finish each word, fill in the missing vowels. Write the complete word on the line.

hdch _____

ct _____

dzznss _____

fvr _____

pn _____

Pick a Word

Underline the word that belongs in each sentence. Then write that word on the line.

An injury can cause _____ .
      optical   pain   pane

A _____ is a sign of illness.
      fever   compass   booster

See a doctor if you have an _____ pain.
      appointment   alcohol   acute

Some drugs cause _____ .
      pharmacy   vaccine   dizziness

A _____ is a pain in the head.
      headset   headache   headline

The blow on his head left him unconscious.

Words and Meanings

Say the medical word out loud and read its meaning. Read the sentence that follows it. Then circle the medical word in the sentence.

Vomiting (VAHM uht ing): *throwing up.*
He began vomiting after he ate the bad food.

Unconscious (uhn KAHN chuhs): *passed out; in a faint.*
The blow on his head left him unconscious.

Infection (in FEK shuhn): *a disease in the body; a sore.*
See a doctor for that infection.

Nausea (NAW zee uh): *feeling sick and wanting to throw up.*
Take this medicine for nausea.

Nervous (NER vuhs): *jumpy; upset.*
I'm so nervous I can't sit down.

Same Words

Check the word in each row that is the same as the first word in the row. Go as fast as you can. Time yourself.

Nausea	Nervous	Nausea	Hernia
Unconscious	Conscious	Unctuous	Unconscious
Vomiting	Vomiting	Voting	Vaccination
Nervous	Nerveless	Nervous	Nausea
Infection	Inspection	Insect	Infection

No. Correct _____

Time _____

43

Word Wheel

Begin at Start. Find the first word. Put a line between it and the next word. Find and mark the other words in the same way. Then write them on the lines below.

_____

_____

_____

_____

_____

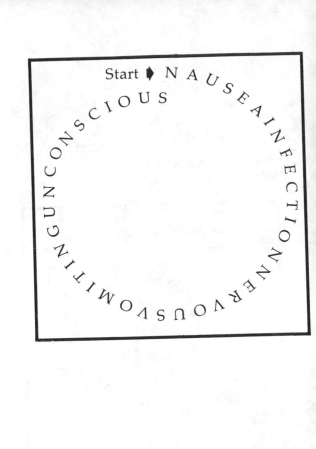

Start ▶ NAUSEAINFECTIONNERVOUSVOMITINGUNCONSCIOUS

Missing Ink

Complete each word by adding the missing parts to each letter. Then write that word on the line.

INFECTION _____

UNCONSCIOUS _____

NAUSEA _____

VOMITING _____

NERVOUS _____

Pick a Word

Underline the word that belongs in each sentence. Then write that word on the line.

He was too _____ to sleep.
        nervous   nurse   elastic

The patient was _____ during
the operation.
    unctuous   compressed   unconscious

She could not eat because of her _____.
    urology   health plan   nausea

He felt sick and began _____.
    nervous   vomiting   infection

If you have an _____, see the doctor.
    therapy   infection   inspection

I'm taking a tablet for this headache.

Words and Meanings

Say the medical word out loud and read its meaning. Read the sentence that follows it. Then circle the medical word in the sentence.

Wound (WOOND): *an injury.*

The wound was bleeding.

Inflammation (in fluh MAY shuhn): *a sore that is red and painful.*

If this ointment causes an inflammation, stop using it.

Capsule (KAP suhl): *a kind of pill.*

The doctor said to take one capsule every day.

Tablet (TAB luht): *a flat pill.*

I'm taking a tablet for this headache.

Addictive (uh DIK tiv): *can't do without; habit-forming.*

Some drugs are addictive.

Same Words

Check the word in each row that is the same as the first word in the row. Go as fast as you can. Time yourself.

Tablet	Tactic	Tablet
Addictive	Additive	Addictive
Capsule	Capsule	Capsize
Wound	Wound	Would
Inflammation	Immunization	Inflammation

No. Correct _____

Time _____

45

Missing Vowels

To finish each word, fill in the missing vowels. Write the complete word on the line.

nflmmtn _____

ddctv _____

wnd _____

tblt _____

cpsl _____

Scrambled Letters

The letters in each word are mixed up. Write the letters so they spell a word from the list at the top of page 45.

atblte _____

downu _____

fnliamamntio _____

ddiaictev _____

pacslue _____

Pick a Word

Underline the word that belongs in each sentence. Then write that word on the line.

Some drugs are _____.
        addictive   additive   fever

A _____ often bleeds.
        fever   headache   wound

The doctor treated the _____.
information   inflammation   immigration

Medicine can come in a _____.
        convulsion   capsule   physical

He took a _____ for his allergy.
        tablet   sinus   tetanus

Review

The 20 words below are hidden in the puzzle. Each word is printed in a straight line. But it may read across, up, down, backwards, or on a slant. Some words overlap. Circle each word as you find it in the puzzle. Then cross it off the list. The first is done.

CHRONIC
COUGH
CONVULSION
EXHAUSTION
BLEEDING
PAIN
ACUTE
FEVER
HEADACHE
DIZZINESS

VOMITING
UNCONSCIOUS
INFECTION
NAUSEA
NERVOUS
WOUND
INFLAMMATION
CAPSULE
TABLET
ADDICTIVE

```
C A V C A P S U L E I B L O
H U C A J A E S U A N L H I
R N E U R V O I S T F E H M
B C B T T W O U N D I E G D
A O G N I E S R E V C D U L
D N I N F L A M M A T I O N
D S D U S S O N E S O N C L
I C H O S R P I T N A E H E
C I Z Z E C H R O N I C L R
T O Z V O M I T I N G A B V
I U Z C O R O U N G H E P O
V S E X H A U S T I O N L U
E F E A D A C H E A S U R S
H E O D C D I Z Z I N E S T
U A D C O N V U L S I O N B
E A C O N V U L S I O N O R
T E L B A T N A D T F O T B
```

Test

Put **+** by each sentence that is true. Put **0** by each sentence that is not true.

_____ 1. An acute pain does not hurt much.

_____ 2. You can take a tablet for a headache.

_____ 3. A chronic cough doesn't last long.

_____ 4. Some drugs are addictive.

_____ 5. A thermometer can show if a person has a fever.

_____ 6. _Exhaustion_ means inflammation.

_____ 7. A person who is having a convulsion can't stop shaking.

_____ 8. _Nausea_ means the same as _nervous_.

_____ 9. A person who is unconscious is awake.

_____ 10. A wound can cause bleeding.

_____ 11. A capsule is a kind of bandage.

_____ 12. Dizziness can sometimes cause a person to fall.

_____ 13. An infection can be a sore.

_____ 14. _Vomiting_ means throwing up.

Guide to Phonetic Respellings*

Many of the words in this book are followed by respellings. The respellings show you how to say the words.

A respelling tells you three things about a word:

1. How many sounds, or syllables, the word has
2. Which syllable to stress
3. How to say each syllable

Look at the chart below. It shows you how to say each part of a respelling.

Now look at the word below. Then look at the respelling that follows it.

example (ig ZAM puhl)

1. How many syllables does *example* have? (3)
2. Which syllable should you stress? (ZAM)
3. How do you say each syllable? (ig) (ZAM) (puhl)

Say **example** (ig ZAM puhl) out loud. Then practice saying these respellings:

practice (PRAK tuhs)   **syllable** (SIL uh buhl)
follow (FAHL oh)   **phonetic** (fuh NET ik)

If you see:	Say it like the:	In:	If you see:	Say it like the:	In:
(a)	a	pat	(m)	m	me
(ah)	a	father	(n)	n	no
(air)	air	fair	(ng)	ng	sing
(aw)	aw	paw	(oh)	oa	coat
(ay)	ay	day	(oi)	oy	boy
(b)	b	bee	(oo)	oo	too
(ch)	ch	chair	(or)	or	for
(d)	d	do	(ow)	ow	how
(e)	e	send	(p)	p	pay
(ee)	ee	see	(r)	r	row
(ehr)	err	merry	(s)	s	say
(er)	er	fern	(sh)	sh	she
(ear)	ear	hear	(t)	t	too
(f)	f	far	(th)	th	thin
(g)	g	go	(*th*)	th	the
(h)	h	he	(u)	u	put
(hw)	wh	where	(uh)	u	but
(i)	i	is	(v)	v	very
(igh)	igh	high	(w)	w	way
(j)	j	joy	(y)	y	you
(k)	k	key	(z)	z	zoo
(l)	l	lay	(zh)	s	treasure

*All respellings are based on pronunciations found in *Webster's New Collegiate Dictionary*, 8th ed. (Springfield, Mass.: G. & C. Merriam Co., 1974). Pronunciations may differ in your community or your geographic region.